So you really want t

English
Prep

BOOK 1

Answer Book

So you really want to learn

English Prep

BOOK 1
Answer Book

Susan Elkin

Series Editor: Nicholas Oulton M.A. (Oxon.)

GALORE PARK

www.galorepark.co.uk

Published by Galore Park Publishing Ltd
PO Box 96, Cranbrook, TN17 4WS
www.galorepark.co.uk

Typography by Typematter, Basingstoke
Printed by The Bath Press

ISBN-10 1 902984 56 0
ISBN-13 978 1 902984 56 8

First published 2005

Accompanying this course:
English Prep Book 1   ISBN 1 902984 53 6
English Prep Book 2   ISBN 1 902984 66 8
English Prep Book 2 Answer book   ISBN 1 902984 57 9

Available in the *So You Really Want to Learn* series:
French
Latin
Spanish
Maths
Science

Introduction

So You Really Want to Learn English Prep Book 1 is intended for use both by teachers and parents. This answer book complements it by suggesting answers to the exercises where appropriate – and makes occasional suggestions about how the book might be used – especially by parents for whom the working methods might be unfamiliar.

Some exercises really don't have, or need, answers. In Chapter 1, Exercise 1.7, for example, pupils are asked to think of various noun-related items and list them. They will come up with a wide range of ideas and none of us can prescribe or predict what these will be. All an assisting adult needs to do is to encourage. And there's quite a lot of that sort of work in *So You Really Want to Learn English Prep Book 1*.

Each chapter begins with two comprehension passages. Ideally a pupil should read the passage through several times and have the opportunity to discuss it with an adult before attempting the questions. It can help for a teacher to read the passage aloud to the pupil first. Or, if he or she can read well enough, the pupil could read it aloud to the teacher and/or the rest of the group. Then a second reading might be a silent one.

I've always found that, with a comprehension exercise, it makes sense to work through the questions orally with the pupil first and then set him/her the task of answering them in writing. Traditionally, comprehension answers are always expressed in complete sentences which repeat part of the question because it reminds pupils of the essential features of a grammatically correct sentence. Some of the answers in this book have been abbreviated.

Don't let's forget this is English, not Maths. Of course there are some questions or items in exercises which have one unarguable answer. But there are many more which do not. Often there are different words which mean something similar and many ways of expressing the same idea. That's part of the joy of English. We want pupils to be original thinkers. So let's encourage them to think as broadly as possible. We don't want to limit them.

It means, though, that quite often my suggested answers need to be mentally prefaced with phrases such as 'words to the effect of ...' or 'something along the lines of ...' There will usually be other, equally appropriate, and perhaps better, ways of putting it.

And sometimes pupils will think of something which I (or you) have not. It always happens in the classroom and it's very encouraging. My answers are not necessarily definitive. Teachers and others working with children have to exercise a bit of humility sometimes. We don't know it all. Far from it.

Each section has a spelling section because, of course, we all want the pupils in our charge to develop into accurate spellers. Remember, though, that it isn't a particularly useful skill to be able to spell a word aloud letter by letter and, for many, it's quite difficult to do because you have to visualise the word first. It is far more important (and generally easier) to learn to write down the words correctly spelled. So when I teach spelling I always get the pupils to write rather than recite.

Teachers of English will have read many of the books I recommend in the 'Have you read ...' sections. So will many parents, but I hope I have made some suggestions which will be new to some adults as well as to children. If you want to encourage a pupil to read there is no substitute for reading the same books and enthusiastically discussing that reading with the pupil. It becomes a shared experience and very special and memorable. This could be yet another way in which parents at home can use *So You Really Want to Learn English Prep Book 1* to develop children's command of English.

So, bearing all that in mind, I hope you find this answer book useful and that it helps the pupils or children you're working with to learn to love English.

SJE
July 2005

Contents

Chapter 1

Exercise 1.1

1. It was three months since the boys had eaten well.

2. The bowls had been licked clean by very hungry boys.

3. Oliver had been chosen by lot.

4. (a) thoroughly, fully, carefully, scrupulously etc.
    (b) positioned, established etc.
    (c) courage, cheek, effrontery, guts etc.
    (d) held, secured etc.

5. Oliver had been hit with a ladle, locked in a dark room for a week, made to wash outdoors in cold water, hit frequently by Mr Bumble while washing and formally beaten in front of other boys at meal times on alternate days.

6. This is to demonstrate the irony, or 'literary sarcasm', in the word 'festive.' It is a hollow joke which is typical of Dickens. The meal is seriously inadequate which is the opposite of festive.

Exercise 1.2

1. (a) 30 boys are likely to be too heavy.
    (b) 25 girls are likely to be too heavy.

2. Possible health problems could include high blood pressure, heart disease and diabetes.

3. Obesity means excessive fatness, fleshiness, corpulence.

4. Obese children may experience low self esteem or low confidence levels.

5. Children can take more exercise and have a healthier diet including fruit and vegetables.

6. If children and adults go on getting fatter there will be an 'explosion' of illness in the population in the future.

7. The Health Promotion Agency hopes teachers, parents, caterers and anyone else who sometimes has responsibility for children's meals such as scout leaders, club organisers etc. will read the notice.

Exercise 1.4

(*Tip:* If pupils read these aloud they can often be helped to get them right instinctively because the voice dips at a full stop.)

1. Life in a Victorian workhouse was very hard. Residents were often hungry.

2. At times Oliver felt very lonely. His mother had died when he was born.

3. Too many British children are obese. Experts think more exercise would help.

4. Oliver asked. The other boys watched.

5. I don't like porridge. My mother does.

Exercise 1.5

Numbers 2, 3, 4, 5 and 7 are complete sentences. Numbers 1, 6 and 8 are not.

2.   Dickens wrote *Oliver Twist*.

3.   Some foods can help to make you too fat.

4.   Oranges are my favourite fruit.

5.   You should always eat your greens.

7.   Pasta is an Italian food.

Numbers 1, 6 and 8 can be completed in almost as many ways as there are children. For example:

1.   *Oliver Twist* and *Nicholas Nickleby*, books by Charles Dickens, are two of my father's favourites.

6.   The two green vegetables I like best are spinach and broccoli.

8.   We often go to the Chinese restaurant near us which serves wonderful sweet and sour vegetables.

Exercise 1.6

Emma has had a bad week. On Monday she was late for school because of a traffic jam. Tuesday was worse. There was rice for lunch. Emma hates rice. On Wednesday she cut her finger on the bread knife at breakfast time.

Things got worse as the week went on. In the supermarket with her mother on Thursday Emma dropped a dozen eggs as she was putting them in the trolley. Then on Friday she fell over the cat and sprained her ankle.

So she went to bed early. On Friday evening she had a nightmare.

Chapter 2

Exercise 2.1

1. Polly stood up and hit her head on a half fallen tree on the bank which knocked her out of the boat.
2. (a) choppiness, swirling etc.
   (b) driven, pushed, forced etc.
   (c) fixed, stuck etc.
3. Roger is terrified and not thinking straight. He tries to look after the boat.
4. Melusine's silent disappearance from the boat. She seems like an invisible underwater animal. She is dry despite having been in the canal.
5. Fright, terror, paralysed, shock, fear, wildly (also squeak, bellowed, desperately, white knuckles, unable to move).
6. The author uses short sentences to maintain the impression of tension and excitement. Things happen faster than words and, by using short sentences, more action can be packed into a smaller space.

Exercise 2.2

1. Dugongs swim slowly using a big tail; they don't need to dive deep to find food; they are rarely attacked by other animals.
2. Sea cows are found in the South West Pacific and Indian Oceans, especially off the tropical coasts of Australia.
3. A shark might attack a dugong.
4. The sea cow sits up in water to suckle babies and makes them look, from a distance, like tailed women.
5. This is indicated by his words 'Some say'.

Exercise 2.4

(*Tip:* If children read these aloud they can often be helped to get them right instinctively because the voice lifts at a question mark.)

(a), (d), (e), (f) and (i) need question marks.

(a) Why wasn't Melusine wet?
(d) What do dugongs eat?
(e) Does the dugong have another name?
(f) How many books has David Attenborough written?
(i) 'Who got me out of the canal?' asked Polly.

Exercise 2.5

Here are fifty words to start you off. Keen pupils will think of many more. You could put a time limit – e.g. 10 minutes – to make it more challenging:

east, main, make, mark, mask, mine, mink, mint, must, nest, note, quake, quirk, quit, quest, question, quote, rain, rake, rest, rink, risk, rote, rust, saint, sake, seam, sink, skin, snore, soak, sore, stank, stark, steam, stem, stink, stir, stone, store, stork, storm, strain, stream, stun, stunk, take, task, team, turn.

Exercise 2.6

The gaps in these sentences are a 'free-for-all' for verbs but here are some possibilities. The pupils will think of others.

1.   Water dripped/fell/cascaded/seeped/trickled from the roof.
2.   Roger pulled/snatched/eased/dragged himself free.
3.   We reached/loved/saw/smelt/left France.
4.   My mother liked/hated/preferred to rest/ride/eat/sunbathe and swim/sleep/sightsee/drive on holiday.
5.   Dugongs live/swim/feed/breed in the sea.
6.   David Attenborough often appears/performs/features on television.
7.   Tomorrow I shall ask/shop/walk/babysit.

Exercise 2.7

It was evening. Polly had been seen by a local doctor who had wanted to take her to hospital in Niort, the nearest large town thirty miles away, but in the end he had agreed that her mother could nurse her at home. He'd bandaged the bump on her head and said that she'd had a very narrow escape from drowning. When he said this, he scowled at her parents in a way that made them both hang their heads like guilty children.

Exercise 2.8

1.   Dogs wag their tails when they're happy.
2.   Roger will moor the boat over there.
3.   There are some cows suckling their young.
4.   Polly and Melusine were both in the water so Roger, their companion, was frightened.
5.   Some mammals live their lives in water.
6.   The trees over there will shed their leaves soon because they're not evergreen.

Chapter 3

Exercise 3.1

1. The child wanted to find out what the crocodile eats for dinner, tired of his grumpy family.

2. No definitive answer – but encourage children to give a full and detailed reason for choice.

3. (a) gathered, collected, amassed etc.
    (b) here
    (c) whipped, beat, thrashed etc.

4. With his new trunk the elephant can swat flies, pluck grass to eat, squirt cooling water on his head, throw his various relations into a wasps' nest or thorn bush, pull out his aunt's tail feathers and blow bubbles to disturb his sleeping aunt.

5. He means 'insatiable curiosity'. It is not certain what he meant instead of provocative: perhaps prohibited – pupils may be able to make other suggestions.

(Such word errors are known as malapropisms after a character in Richard Brinsley Sheridan's 18th century play *The Rivals*. Mrs Malaprop makes hilarious mistakes in almost every sentence. Pupils might enjoy learning about this and why malapropisms are so called.)

Exercise 3.2

1. Rob Atkinson is Head of the Wildlife Department of the RSPCA.

2. The head office is based in Horsham, West Sussex.

3. He thinks it is cruel because it shortens their life expectancy; the enclosures are too small; they have a poor diet; they suffer more illness; they are often in an inappropriate social grouping; they can suffer ill-treatment by keepers etc.

4. The cost of housing elephants properly in European zoos is very high.

5. He would prefer the money to be spent on conservation in the wild.

6. He wrote the letter as a response to an article by Richard Morrison a week earlier.

7. (a) inadequate, poor etc.
    (b) low, unsatisfactory etc.
    (c) expensive, costly, off-putting etc.

Exercise 3.4

1. Elephants like to eat melons, bananas, leaves, grasses and other plants.

2. The elephant's nose was tugged, yanked, dragged, heaved and stretched by the crocodile.

3. Near the river bank lay a clever, talkative, helpful and knowledgeable python.

4. Should elephants, lions, tigers, gorillas and bears be kept in zoos?

5. You could ask your mother, father, sister, brother, aunt or uncle what they think.

Exercise 3.5

This is how you could do this exercise if you use the words provided. Pupils are free to come up with other ideas. It is important that they 'fence off' (parenthesise) their inserts with pairs of commas.

1. The elephant's child, you see, was insatiably curious.
2. His relations, however, refused to answer questions patiently.
3. Nearby, on the banks of the Limpopo, a frantic struggle took place.
4. Listen, my child, and I'll tell you a story.
5. If you want advice, remember, ask a rock-snake.

Exercise 3.6

3.

Noun	Adjective
obedience	obedient
thickness	thick
success	successful
curiosity	curious
naughtiness	naughty
circle	circular
picture	picturesque

Chapter 4

Exercice 4.1

1. The author uses adjectives such as 'bleak' and 'ugly'; there is an emphasis within his description on emptiness and impenetrability; the use of the words 'funny' and 'foreign' describing the smell in the woods; Chas has always considered the wood as 'oddly discouraging'.

2. The first sign is the smell of burning and petrol.

3. Chas wants to get the machine gun.

4. Chas sees the gunner, apparently intact, still sitting in the cockpit as if alive. Then he realises that the gunner is dead. This adds to the tension and immediacy in the writing.

5. The body of the aircraft is on the laundry roof, the tail is on the ground.

6. (a) woven, patterned etc.
   (b) looked, gazed etc.
   (c) take back, handle again etc.

Exercice 4.2

1. Utility clothing was low cost clothing introduced by the government when materials became very expensive during the war. Almost no materials could be imported.

2. People used to patch and darn their clothes.

3. Thermojene was insulating material worn inside clothing.

4. The 'points' system was intended to introduce fairness; the government didn't want some people to have more than others when there wasn't sufficient to go round.

5. Chas probably would have worn short trousers, a shirt, a pullover, a jacket and long socks. (The description says he was wearing plimsolls on his feet. It's winter.)

Exercice 4.4

1. (a) Stop thief!
   (b) What a terrible story!
   (c) How hot the weather is!
   (d) You poor child!
   (e) What a shame!
   (f) How lovely!

2. (a) He wanted to find the source of the smell.
   (b) How few clothes those children had in the 1940s!
   (c) No, don't do that!
   (d) Most girls wore berets.
   (e) Mending clothes made them last.
   (f) What a smell!
   (g) Ouch!

Exercise 4.5

Pupils can put any adverbs which seem appropriate in these gaps. It's a free choice – but here are some suggestions.

1. (a) Chas McGill entered the wood excitedly/cautiously/apprehensively and searched carefully/thoroughly/casually for souvenirs.
    (b) During the war everyone had to dress practically/cheaply/simply.
    (c) Many people are now very/deeply/passionately interested in the Second World War.
    (d) Children in the war were usually/sensibly advised to keep away from aircraft and weapons.
    (e) Some older people often/sometimes remember Second World War bombing raids clearly/distinctly.
    (f) Rationing was a way of sharing things out fairly/equitably/evenly.

2.

Adjective	Adverb
normal	normally
good	well
funny	funnily
bad	badly
expensive	expensively
frightening	frighteningly
public	publicly
clear	clearly
warm	warmly
easy	easily

Chapter 5

Exercise 5.1

1. The differences he notices are the trees and fields, horse drawn traffic, and that there are no office buildings.
2. James Burbage built The Theatre in Shoreditch.
3. The theatre could no longer be used as the lease had expired.
4. (a) destruction/breaking/dismantling etc.
    (b) mouldy/stale/dusty etc.
5. You need to cross the River Thames via London Bridge.
6. The people have strange accents; they are wearing Elizabethan clothes as if they are on a film set.

Exercise 5.2

1. At the time of writing this book (2005) the Globe has been open for eight years. The Globe was opened in 1997 so calculate from the current year.
2. The most difficult part of his job was designing the stage and the dressing room.
3. McCurdy had made a good impression on Sam Wanamaker with his work on Barley Hall in York.
4. Most of the work was done in Berkshire, in McCurdy's workshops.
5. The structure was built on an oak frame including columns 28 feet high supporting a 16 tonne roof. The design includes a stage and dressing space, modelled closely on the 16th century Globe Theatre.
6. The Globe is now a theatre and tourist attraction. It does research, educational work and drama training.

Exercise 5.4

1. Pupils will think of lots of examples e.g. fussiness, tidiness, laziness, silliness, sleepiness.
2. There are plenty of possibilities here too, e.g.

merry	merriment
grumpy	grumpiness
hefty	heftiness
salty	saltiness
easy	ease/easiness
soppy	soppiness

3. (a) The Globe is a careful replica of an Elizabethan building.
    (b) We can understand the popularity of Elizabethan drama.
    (c) Nat Field was surprised by the atmosphere of Tudor London.
    (d) Shakespeare was English.
    (e) Oak is a very hard and reliable wood.

Exercise 5.5

1. We put on a play with a five-person cast.

2. James I of England was a non-smoker.

3. In Shakespeare's play *Hamlet*, Claudius is Gertrude's brother-in-law as well as her new husband and Hamlet's stepfather.

4. *Henry V* by Shakespeare, written in 1599, was a turn-of-the-century play.

5. Queen Victoria's end-of-reign celebration was her Diamond Jubilee in 1897 when she had been monarch for 60 years.

6. Shakespeare lived in Stratford-upon-Avon.

Exercise 5.6

1. The Globe Theatre was magnificent – but it burned down.

2. Shakespeare's *Macbeth* was very ambitious – although audiences usually think he was led on by his wife.

3. Sam Wanamaker worked for years on the Globe Theatre project – but died before it was finished.

4. Queen Elizabeth encouraged playwrights – but she never went to the theatre.

Chapter 6

Exercise 6.1

1. The minotaur was large and heavy – nearly three metres tall. It was very muscular. It had the upper body of a man, and the lower body of a bull – but with a powerful bull's head, including menacing horns. The minotaur was fierce with fangs and yellow eyes and a swinging tail. It was covered with sweat, mud (or excrement) and dried blood and a terrifying roar.

2. (a) minimal/thin/pale etc.
    (b) spiked/pinned/speared etc.
    (c) fires/stoves etc.

3. The narrative says he sees the minotaur's body, eyes, horns and size, he hears its hooves clashing and its bellow, he smells sweat, mud etc. and incense, and he feels the slimy floor, the stone columns and the heat of the braziers.

4. Phoenix felt disorientated, relieved, exhilarated, excited, frightened and proud.

5. The row of noughts indicates a nil score. Phoenix was defeated in the game because he ran away.

6. Phoenix is playing a 'virtual reality' computer game where you pit yourself against an enemy.

Exercise 6.2

1. Part 2 ends at 10.10 pm.

2. Anna Maxwell Martin plays the part of Lyra.

3. The list of adjectives are: epic, filmic, dramatic, remarkable, outstanding, assured, mercurial, gravelly, crisp, atmospheric, successful, moving, profound, entertaining.

    The list of adverbs are: splendidly, imaginatively, richly, lithely, effectively, sensitively, immaculately, and gloriously.

4. She did not like Niamh Cusack's limited voice range and Timothy Dalton's wooden, sometimes inaudible performance.

5. The daemons are depicted by puppets operated by actors dressed in black who shadow the main actors.

6. The Olivier Theatre has a moving circular stage ('revolve') which allows rapid high-tech scene change on several planes.

Exercise 6.4

1. (a) C'bury   (vii)   Canterbury
    (b) can't   (v)   cannot
    (c) let's   (vi)   let us
    (d) P'boro   (iii)   Peterborough
    (e) there's   (ii)   there is (or there has)
    (f) you'll   (viii) you will (or you shall)
    (g) who's   (iv)   who is (or who has)
    (h) isn't   (i)   is not

2. Abigail knew she'd have to hurry. She'd been told to get to the shop before it shut at six o'clock. 'We've run out of salt,' she told Mr Evans, the corner shopkeeper. 'We're having fish and chips for supper and it'd be horrible without salt.'

Exercise 6.5

1. Timothy Dalton's script.
2. The Minotaur's huge horns.
3. My brother's computer game.
4. Phoenix's father.
5. Nicholas Wright's play.
6. The boys' big bag of crisps (several boys, one bag).
7. The princess's coat (one princess).
8. The princesses' sister (several princesses, one sister).

Exercise 6.6

1. Examples:

cold	colder	coldest
hot	hotter	hottest
sad	sadder	saddest
cruel	crueller	cruellest
entertaining	more entertaining	most entertaining
amusing	more amusing	most amusing

etc.

2. (a) The koala bear is the sweetest little bear in the world. (Point of accuracy – actually, although this is the sort of thing people say and write so it's useful as an exercise, the koala is not a bear at all. It's a marsupial, like the kangaroo and wallaby.)
    (b) London is more crowded than Edinburgh.
    (c) *Shadow of the Minotaur* is the most exciting fantasy I have read.
    (d) The Olivier is one of London's largest theatres.
    (e) *His Dark Materials* is the best thing Philip Pullman has written.
    (f) This slave girl is pretty, this one is quite attractive, but this one over here is by far the most beautiful.

Exercise 6.7

This is a creative task and the pupils will think, we hope, of imaginative ways of using the given words. These are just examples.

1. So eloquent was our teacher when she talked about Philip Pullman's books that we all went straight to the library to borrow them.
    Eloquent and convincing, our member of parliament was re-elected.

2. 'You are loquacious but I wish you were eloquent,' our teacher told the ever-talkative Peter.

   In a play a very loquacious person, who would be boring in real life, can be very funny because we laugh at his or her constant, meaningless chatter.

3. A ventriloquist is a kind of puppeteer who projects his voice so that we think the puppet is talking.

   Rod Hull was such a fine ventriloquist that when Emu spoke you couldn't see Hull's lips moving.

Chapter 7

Exercise 7.1

1. It would have taken them roughly three minutes to walk to the sea.

2. Flora's mother will unpack while they are out.

3. Flora is most frightened of snakes and scorpions – they might get in her footwear.

4. She regrets her treatment of the jellyfish as they looked vulnerable when dead and she wouldn't want to be prodded if she were dead.

5. Flora is wearing socks with her sandals and she likens the waves on the sand to skirts frilled with white crochet. The language between the parents and Flora is slightly stilted with a 1950s ring e.g. 'She's tired dear', and the child's careful use of subjunctive in 'If I were dead.' There is no slang or casual language. The word 'nasties' is a bit old-fashioned. The conversation is more formal than that of most 21st century families.

6. It is dusk for only a very short time.

7. Insect noise and her mother shutting up for the night keep Flora awake.

Exercise 7.2

1. The tour will finish on 26th March.

2. The adjectives are: great, fascinating, uncommercialised, relaxing, enchanting, tropical, exquisite, blue, dramatic, perfumed, lush, mysterious.

3. Using 'Odyssey' sounds more glamorous and romantic. It is associated with the hot, sunny Mediterranean because, in Greek mythology, that's where Odysseus made his journey.

4. The minimum cost is £4,800.

5. France once governed most of the islands.

6. (a) unspoiled, undeveloped etc.
    (b) embodiment, ideal example etc.
    (c) taste, try, sample, enjoy etc.

Exercise 7.4

There is more than one way of using conjunctions to join these sentences. These suggestions are just examples.

1. Tigers live in India but lions are native to Africa.

2. My little sister is hungry so we must have lunch soon.

3. Dolphins are mammals although they swim like fish.

4. We must hurry to the classroom or we shall be late.

5. Ants live in colonies and work together.

6. A python is not a dangerous animal to human beings, but don't interfere with it.

7. Most of the buildings are air-conditioned because it is very hot in Hong Kong.

8. Marcus is in the choir and his sister plays hockey in the school team.

Exercise 7.5

1. (a) comma
    (b) apostrophe
    (c) dash
    (d) hyphen
    (e) full stop

2. (a) comma
    (b) dash
    (c) apostrophe
    (d) brackets
    (e) full stop
    (f) question mark

Exercise 7.6

Encourage the pupils to use these words freely. These suggestions are just examples:

The sea urchin is a most interesting **marine** creature.

I went to the Red Sea with my family for diving and other **aquatic** sports.

Sailors are sometime called **mariners** because they sail on the sea.

My bicycle tyre has a **puncture** where it was penetrated by a nail in the road.

We watched the sharks from a **submarine** observation capsule.

A **punctual** person arrives exactly on time.

Chapter 8

Exercise 8.1

1.   He kept the spells in his large and well-proportioned house on the Nile, inside a black ebony box bound with silver and gold bands.

2.   (a)   vengeance, to get his own back etc.
      (b)   deprived, widowed (in this context)
      (c)   call, signal etc.
      (d)   regret, sorrow etc.

3.   The crocodile was very large, muscular and white, with a long muzzle and fierce interlocking teeth.

4.   He was jealous of the other man. He was made to look silly and he was disappointed.

5.   King Nebka regarded Uba-na-ner as basically a good man and he knew that he was sorry.

Exercise 8.2

1.   Coriander and cumin are used in falafel.

2.   Most frying pans are not large enough to take all the falafel at once.

3.   Yes, you could offer it to a vegetarian as it contains no meat, fish, poultry or any of their by-products.

4.   You can see falafel being eaten on the streets of Cairo.

5.   The mixture is rolled in the palms of your hands.

6.   It is cooked when it is brown on both sides.

Exercise 8.4

1.   A Traditional tale affects many readers

2.   Falafel makes fingers sticky

3.   Uba-na-ner watched the big crocodile

4.   King Nebka forgave Uba-na-ner.

5.   Nicola ate her falafel.

Exercise 8.5

1.   1.   Many readers are affected by a traditional tale.
      2.   Sticky fingers are made by falafel.
      3.   The big crocodile was watched by Uba-na-ner.
      4.   Uba-na-ner was forgiven by King Nebka.
      5.   Falafel were eaten by Nicola

2. The following are just example answers. Pupils will complete these sentences in different ways.
    (a) Uba-na-ner's fiancée was attracted by another man. (passive)
    (b) My cooking is improving. (active)
    (c) Take-away shops in Cairo are used by office workers. (passive)
    (d) Falafel is a traditional Arabic dish. (active)
    (e) A piece of white wax was shaped into a crocodile by the angry man. (passive)
    (f) The magician was jilted by his intended bride. (passive)
    (g) Crocodiles no longer live in the lower Nile but only south of Aswan. (active)
    (h) Egyptians are admired by the rest of the world for their long history. (passive)

3. Here are some more sample answers – encourage the pupils to be as imaginative as possible. The subjects of these sentence are underlined. Don't forget that if there is a preposition (e.g. Ships sail **on** the River Nile) then the sentence is using an **indirect object** and that's a different story. So no prepositions here, please!
    (a) <u>We</u> all enjoyed the story.
    (b) <u>Fiona</u> could see the River Nile.
    (c) <u>The prime minister</u> condemned their bad behaviour.
    (d) <u>My mother</u> hates the smell of falafel frying.
    (e) <u>His fiancée</u> abandoned Uba-na-ner.
    (f) <u>Harry Potter</u> knows plenty of magic spells.

Exercise 8.6

The following suggestions are examples, not answers:

1. These are a few of my favourite things: donkeys, lilies, velvet and anything lilac-coloured or smelling of freesia.

2. My Latin teacher taught us verbs in the following way: she gave us instructions in Latin and made us carry out the action, stating, in Latin, what we were doing, so that we learned several parts of the verb.

3. The mother said to the child: 'Go out and explore.'

Puzzle

Answer to puzzle: princes, princess.

Chapter 9

Exercise 9.1

1. Falls were worse if both crutches slipped backward because these winded him, threw him forward and twisted his bad leg.

2. The child with mobility difficulties admires the effortless locomotion of the dog, resulting in empathy and envy. There is a contrast with himself but no bitterness.

3. He says that the falls 'did not distress me'; they were a 'part of normal living' (lines 15-16). He didn't think of himself as a cripple, and in line 19 he refers to cripples and their constant concern in the 3rd person.

4. (a) rub, irritate etc.
   (b) divert, go out of my way etc.
   (c) looping, lolloping etc.
   (d) exciting, forward looking, eager etc.

5. The bush, kangaroo dog, frogs in the swamp and possums.

6. He took the shortest route. He needed to find ways of living a normal life despite his disability.

Exercise 9.2

1. (a) framework, foundation etc.
   (b) hard, strong etc.
   (c) thigh bone

2. The skeleton carries your weight, keeps you upright and provides an anchorage for your muscles.

3. The skeleton is misnamed by the Greeks who thought the skeleton was dry, as in a long-dead body. If a body is alive, its bone is living, growing tissue.

4. Calcium phosphate gives bones their strength.

5. There are more than 200 bones in the body, so you need to multiply 200 by the number in the class. In a class of 20 the answer is roughly 4,000. In a class of 25 it would be roughly 5,000 and so on.

Exercise 9.4

1. The children protested when they were told off.

2. Emma's father asked her to help her disabled brother.

3. The headmaster asked the teachers to come to his office when they had dismissed their classes.

4. The mayoress said she had a severe headache.

5. The blind man said he used a guide dog.

6. Raj took one look at the calculator and saw that it was his.

Exercise 9.5

1. The new caravan is theirs.

2. Is that red scarf hers?

3. This wheelchair is mine.

4. The responsibility is yours.

5. This is our home.

Exercise 9.6

1. It's a pity that it's raining today.

2. The skeleton in the science lab has lost its labels.

3. What a long day it's been.

4. It's necessary to visit a museum to find out about its history.

5. Ask anyone in the school to tell you about its rules.

Exercise 9.7

1. Perry and I are going to learn the names of all the bones in the body.

2. Jasmine, who is profoundly deaf, invited Ella and me to her party.

3. There was trouble ahead for Guy and me.

4. Uncle John sent presents for James and me.

5. Clearly Felix and I were in trouble because he had lost his crutches.

6. Mrs Burns grumbled at Jake and me for being late.

Exercise 9.8

1. 'Is it morning already?' asked Joshua, sitting up in bed.

2. 'Oh please let me go,' pleaded Peter.

3. Dad announced: 'As soon as Mrs Methuen says "Good morning" I shall be going out.'

4. 'Do you know,' said Jack, 'that the collar bone is called the clavicle?'

5. 'My address,' said Mr Micawber, 'is Windsor Terrace, City Road.'

Exercise 9.9

The field is wide open with this one! Some possibilities include:

1. Simple: difficult, hard, complex, complicated.

2. Easy: stiff, uneasy, awkward.

3. Sad: happy, cheerful, light-hearted, ebullient.

4. Bright: dull, matt, unintelligent, cloudy.

5. Dark: light, fair, blond(e).

6. Funny: serious, grave, straight, unfunny.

Chapter 10

Exercise 10.1

1. (a)   12th April 1939 (approximately).
    (b)   29th August 1939 (approximately).

2. Ossie is Billy's coach, adviser, family friend and father figure. Later he becomes his stepfather.

3. Ossie didn't want him to get conceited and stop concentrating on playing better.

4. Billy needed to focus on the game and resist being dazzled by the thought of playing for a famous club.

5. Billy felt proud, thrilled, excited and pleased to be praised in newspapers.

6. The Chelsea shirt was blue at this time.

7. Billy uses phrase such as 'for a while at least'; 'but it disappeared like everything else'; and 'another thing I hadn't seen coming.'

Exercise 10.2

1. Jonny Wilkinson scored the winning goal.

2. Other England players are: Martin Johnson, Jason Robinson, Ben Kay, Will Greenwood, Lawrence Dallaglio, Richard Hill.

3. Extra time was played because a kick from Elton Flatley made the scores even.

4. This game was exciting because England had nearly won. There were two sloppy penalties given away by England which brought Australia close to their score, then Wilkinson missed a drop goal. Just as England thought they had recovered, Elton Flatley's kick pushed the match into extra time. With 26 seconds of extra time left to play, Wilkinson scored his winning penalty.

5. The writer supports England which is clear from the following phrases: 'mighty England pack'; 'soon silenced strong home support'; 'were not to be denied'; 'deserved victory'; and 'memorable result'.

Exercise 10.4

We **were** waiting for the bus. We didn't mind whether it **was** a red, green or blue bus. We were prepared to take the first one which came. The centre of the town **was** our destination. My eldest sister **was** going to a wedding and she **was** planning to buy a really special outfit. Determined as she **was** to buy something extravagant and colourful, we **were** sure she would buy something black and dreary because that's what she always does. However none of us **was** right.

(*Note:* Mind this one – the subject of the sentence is 'none' which is singular (short for no one).)

She eventually chose a bright pink suit which she **was** going to wear with a lime green blouse and scarlet hat. Everybody **was** trying to dissuade her, but unfortunately we **were** unsuccessful. She was all set to go to the wedding looking like a parrot.

Exercise 10.5

1. Fleet of ships.

2. Host of angels.

3. Chest of drawers.

4. Swarm of insects.

5. Peal of bells.

6. Gang of thieves.

7. Choir of singers.

8. Bunch of grapes.

Note: Some copies of English Prep Book 1 show item (h) as thieves or pilgrims. Thieves and pilgrims do not, of course, share a collective noun. In the re-prints of the book 'or pilgrims' has been omitted.

Exercise 10.6

1. The hockey team is triumphant after its win.

2. The hockey players are nervous about their match.

3. Everyone in the team is delighted.

4. The school's swimming relay team is looking forward to the gala.

5. Are the musicians confident about the concert?

6. The wolf pack is howling.

7. The choir is on top form.

8. Everybody is pleased.

Exercise 10.7

These suggestions are just examples.

1. My sister plays squash with its driving speed, which she finds exhilarating; badminton, when she's in the mood for something gentler; tennis because she loves the open air, the smell of grass and the summer atmosphere of tennis whites and strawberries; and table tennis on wet or wintry days because she's very determined to keep her hand in with racquet sports.

2. The most popular sports on television are football, traditional, solid and part of our culture; tennis because the court fits so readily onto the screen and people adore Wimbledon; cricket, associated with willow, leather and village life; and snooker because when colour television was invented in the 1960s viewers could see what was happening and snooker acquired a new following.

3. I like swimming because it gives a feeling of strength and freedom; ice-skating, elegant and individual; ballet as you need music and I'm a sucker for all that gorgeous Tchaikovsky and Delibes; and riding, another sport I can do without being in a team.

Exercise 10.8

1. Our first eleven beat Millford School by two goals to one.

2. It was too hot even to play tennis so we sat and ate two ice creams each.

3. Two boys played two girls at table tennis in a game which the boys were surprised to lose.

4. Lacrosse is popular but lots of pupils like hockey too.

5. I am going to work on cricketing skills this year, especially bowling.

6. My two friends and I have all been chosen to swim for the school.